LINNEA

Copyright © 2022 by Stephanie Emanuel

All rights reserved. This book or any portion thereof may not be reproduced or used in any manner whatsoever without the express written permission of the publisher except for the use of brief quotations in a book review.

Printed in the United States of America

First Printing, 2022

ISBN: 978-0-578-27479-9

HEIGHTS CREMATORY

Cremated Remains of:
Linnea Pionke

By the order of:
HEIGHTS CREMATORY

Date of Cremation:
11-4-19

DEDICATION: To Linnea Pionke

LINNEA

By Stephanie Emanuel

LINNEA

Once upon a time, there was a little girl. Her name was Linnea. Linnea loved animals, the beach and relaxing. When Linnea was little, she lived in Malta, Illinois, a little town West of Chicago. Malta is not far from N.I.U. Her mother, Doris Ada Goble, married Carl Arthur Palm. Carls parents were immigrants from Sweden.

Linneas family celebrated May Day and Sweetest Day every year. Sweetest Day is always celebrated on the third Saturday of October. It's a day to say "thank you" to the special people in your life. It's a day of good deeds.

May Day is a European festival of ancient origins marking the beginning of summer, usually celebrated on May 1st.

One of the traditions is the May Day basket. This was popular back in the 19th and 20th centuries. First, people would fill paper baskets, or cones with treats and flowers. Then, they'd knock on the door and yell "May basket"! and run away. If they got caught, the gifter owed the giftee a kiss.

Linneas family gave little baskets of treats, to friends and family members. When Linnea had her own children, Stephanie, Heather, and James, they were not forgotten. The tradition continues, as of today, Stephanie, Linneas oldest daughter celebrates Sweetest Day and May Day with her children.

Linnea grew up loving animals. She had a pet squirrel named Sammy. She would dress Sammy up and feed Sammy. Sammy was a baby squirrel. that lived in the house.

As Linnea grew older and had her own home, she wanted a pet. She went to the animal shelter while living in Florida, and searched for a pet. There were so many to see. It was very overwhelming and upsetting, to see so many sad animals needing homes.

Waking through the shelter, she came across an orange tabby cat. She was very interested in him. Linnea wanted to take him home. She knew he was the one that needed her.

That same day, Linnea went to the animal shelter, was the day she brought Garfleld home with her. Linnea loved Garfield so much! She wanted to surprise her son Jimmy, with a cat Garfield was loved by them so much! Garfield had lots of treats, toys and the best litter. He was able to lay on the couch, beds, anywhere he wanted.

Garfield eventually got older and passed away. It was a very devastating day. Then, something came to Linnea. She thought to keep him forever, she had to do something. But, what could she do? She loved him so much, she didn't want to let him go. Garfield had been in the family over 20 years.

Linnea decided, she needed him stuffed. She found a taxidermy service in Florida. It took Linnea awhile to come up with the funds for Garfield. He was not allowed to go home with her, until the full payment was made.

Stephanie, Linneas daughter, helped her with the rest of the funds for Garfield. Stephanie continued to communicate with the taxidermist until, he was finally shipped to her, while living in Illinois. Then Garfield arrived! Lots of joyful tears.

Linnea loved relaxing, whether it was by the fireplace, having a steak dinner by candlelight, laying on the beach, feeling the warm sunshine on her face, or relaxing on the couch, under a warm blanket. having a warm cup of coffee, on a cold breezy winter day. Linneas couch, had a piece of fabric, with palm trees printed all over it, very comforting.

Linnea loved the beach! The water is so mesmerizing to her. Listening to the sound of the waves, watching the boats glide through the water, laying on the beach in the sand, with the sun shinning on her golden blonde hair, close to the swaying palm trees.

Linnea heard John Mellencamp, Hurts So Good, along with Lionel Richie, All Night Long, (Stephanies favorite), and many more classics, not far away, playing at the World Famous Elbo Room, in Fort Lauderdale, Florida.

Linnea was not a stranger to the World Famous Elbo Room, she had a few drinks with Stephanie one night, where Stephanie ended up being carried out. Somehow she lost one shoe, and ended up with a man's blue slip on shoe. Linnea said, "you should of talked to him, he' s a pilot".

Linnea later developed cancer, she was on her 5th cancer. Cancer had taken the life of her mother, as well as her niece. She handled the situation very well, considering all of the pain and problems that occurred.

Then, it just became too much, it would mean, she would end up on a ventilator, the rest of her life, being fed through a feeding tube. That is not what she would of wanted.

Linnea would always pray at 11:11 whether morning or evening. Her alarm was always set. She believed 11:11 was a lucky number. This would keep her going.

Linneas daughter Stephanie, had always been there to rescue her, Just like the day she was transferred to an assisted living facility, Seaview. She spoke to Stephanie on the phone to discuss the care she was receiving, or to mention not receiving.

As Stephanie approached her floor, the elevator door opened. There was a very bad, strong odor throughout the floor. She then continued to her mothers room. Stephanie knew something was wrong.

Linnea was in the process of packing up her few things she had. Linnea said, "let's go for a walk, OUTSIDE!" She approached the elevator with Stephanie. Linnea was stopped as they both continued to the car, walking along the sidewalk.

Linnea was asked, "where are you going?" "are you coming back?" The answer came as "no!"

Linnea passed away on July 9th 2019, in Chicago Illinois. Her daughter Stephanie was living in Florida at the time. She flew from Florida to Chicago on November 4th, 2019. Stephanie brought with her a turquoise crochet blanket, she had been making for her.

She was able to speak to Linnea, and cover her with the crochet blanket she made for her, before she was cremated.

The ashes were very warm, they continued to be warm, days and weeks later. Surprisingly, you could see very small pieces of the turquoise crochet blanket, mixed in with Linneas ashes.

Linneas daughter Stephanie, took her to see her mother and father, where they are buried In Malta, Illinois. She then took her to her favorite Mexican restaurant Rositas in Dekalb, Illinois, where she recently resided. Linnea sat in the third booth from the wall, on the left side, facing the drink station, it was the inner seat on the right side, as you walk in the now front door.

Stephanie took Linnea back with her to Florida the next morning. She was placed on a pink crochet blanket. Stephanie had two rabbits. She let the rabbits run around in the living room, near Linnea. She put out a cup of coffee, along with a sweet treat for breakfast, such as, a piece of coffee cake, her favorite! Stephanie placed it next to her, while placing her in the sunshine.

Stephanie had noticed, that her white watch had stopped. It was dead, needlng another battery, but then, she noticed the hands on the clock. The hands were pointed to 11:11 with a date of 2. Stephanie realized that's the exact time that Linnea had prayed. The two could of been, the 2nd of July, a week before Linnea passed away. With this conformation, Stephanie believes Linnea will always be with her.

On December 26th, 2019, Stephanie took Linnea to an Island. There were dolphins, pelicans, palm trees, bunnies hopping around, boats gliding through the water, and thousands of colorful sea shells. There's even a fishing pier with a lighthouse.

After Linnea was carefully placed on the Island, it started raining. Stephanie said, her goodbyes. The second she said, her goodbyes, a rainbow appeared, not only one rainbow, but two rainbows. Stephanie knew this was a really good day, as for the ending conformation of the two rainbows! She felt this was Linneas way of saying "thank-you" and "I love you!"

As of today, Stephanie is working as a nurse. She's trying to make changes, to the nursing facility, Linnea had been admitted to. She has visited Linnea a few times, since being placed at her final resting place. She will continue to visit her mother on the island, as she had a visit on Linneas Birthday, November 4th Linnea can finally rest in peace, and have no more pain!

Linnea has taught me, Stephanie Lee, if someone takes something from you, maybe they needed it more than you. In addition to have fun! Continue traditions, love nature, our animals, relax, and take time for yourself. R.I.P. Linnea Maureen Pionke 11-04-1953 to 07-09-2019. We all love you! We will miss your sense of humor and creativity.

www.ingramcontent.com/pod-product-compliance
Lightning Source LLC
Chambersburg PA
CBHW042046290426
44109CB00001B/44